A-10 Warthog Mini in action

By Ken Neubeck

Color by Don Greer
& Tom Tullis

Illustrated by Joe Sewell

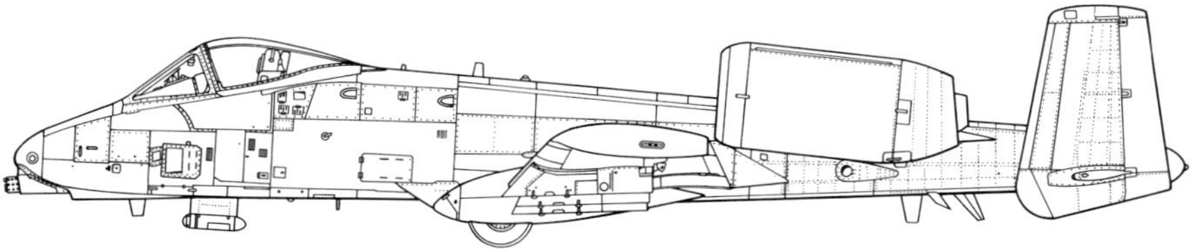

Mini Number 4

squadron/signal publications

An A-10A Warthog of the 23rd Tactical Fighter Wing attacks Iraqi armor in Kuwait during Operation DESERT STORM.

Acknowledgements

Anthony Abbott
Jim Boss (Cradle of Aviation)
Dave Conroe
Fairchild-Republic Archives
John Golden
Elliot Kazan
Ken Kubik
Rick Llinares (Flight Line Photography
Michael Prolab
Robert Pease
Tony Sacketos
Fred Schenkler III
Joshua Stoff (Cradle of Aviation)
Willa Talon (Public Affairs, 23 TFW)
USAF

The YA-10 prototype during flight testing at Edwards AFB, California. Fairchild-Republic made the YA-10s as close to production standard as possible, which was a major factor in the Air Force choosing the A-10 as the winner of the AX fly-off. (Fairchild-Republic)

ISBN 0-89747-335-3

If you have any photographs of aircraft, armor, soldiers or ships of any nation, particularly wartime snapshots, why not share them with us and help make Squadron/Signal's books all the more interesting and complete in the future. Any photograph sent to us will be copied and the original returned. The donor will be fully credited for any photos used. Please send them to

Если у вас есть фотографии самолётов, вооружения, солдат или кораблей любой страны, особенно, снимки времён войны, поделитесь с нами и помогите сделать новые книги издательства Эскадрон/Сигнал ещё интереснее. Мы переснимем ваши фотографии и вернём оригиналы. Имена приславших снимки будут сопровождать все опубликованные фотографии. Присылайте, пожалуйста, фотографии по адресу:

軍用機、装甲車両、兵士、軍艦などの写真を所持しておられる方はいらっしゃいませんか？どの国のものでも結構です。作戦中に撮影されたものが特に良いのです。Squadron/Signal社の出版する刊行物において、このような写真は内容を一層充実し、興味深くすることができます。当方にお送り頂いた写真は、複写の後お返しいたします。出版物中に写真を使用した場合は、必ず提供者のお名前を明記させて頂きます。お写真は下記にご送付ください。

Squadron/Signal Publications, Inc.
1115 Crowley Drive
Carrollton, TX 75011-5010 USA

11369
U.S. AIR FORCE

Introduction

As a result of its experience with the problems of providing ground support in Vietnam, along with the existing Soviet threat in Europe, particularly their superiority in armor, the Air Force determined that there was a need for specialized Close Air Support (CAS) aircraft. After a number of trade studies were conducted and requirements determined, bids were submitted to the Air Force by six aircraft companies during the Spring of 1970. One of the companies that bid on this proposal was the Fairchild-Republic company.

Even prior to bidding on the CAS contract, the Fairchild-Republic Company was a company rich in aviation history and traditions. As the name implies, Fairchild-Republic was the marriage of two aviation companies. The merger took place in 1965 with both companies having played a big part of aviation history, much of it occurring on Long Island, New York, a major center for both military and commercial aircraft. The Republic Aviation Corporation had built a long line of fighter aircraft for the USAF, beginning with the P-47 Thunderbolt for the United States Army Air Force during the Second World War, the F-84 Thunderjet which saw action in Korea, and the F-105 Thunderchief which saw duty in Vietnam. By the end of 1964; however, the Republic company was in financial difficulty and it merged with the Fairchild-Hiller Company the following year. When the new Fairchild-Republic Company failed to win the FX contract (later to become the F-15) during 1966, it was in danger of closing its doors on Long Island. It was at this point that the company was selected to bid on the CAS contract, known at this time as the AX program, which was targeted as a "must win" for the company.

On 18 December 1970, Fairchild-Republic and the Northrop Company were selected by the Air Force as the two companies to participate in a competitive prototype development and flyoff for the AX program. They were the only two companies of the six to propose turbofan engines for their designs and this was a major factor in their selection. Fairchild would receive a contract worth some 41 million dollars for two prototypes to be used in the competitive flyoff evaluation, while Northrop was given 23 million dollars. The difference in money awarded resulted from a bold move on Fairchild's part in that they would develop an aircraft that was as close to production standard as possible, while the Northrop design was strictly a conventional prototype that would have required several changes before going into production. This was a calculated risk that Fairchild-Republic was taking, since

Fairchild-Republic personnel put the final touches on the prototype YA-10 prior to its disassembly for shipment to Edwards Air Force Base, California for a fly-off against the Northrop A-9. (Fairchild-Republic)

The YA-10 prototype is rolled out of the main hangar at the Fairchild-Republic plant on 22 April 1972 for shipment to Edwards Air Force Base, California. (Fairchild-Republic)

funds for a new development contract are generally tight. In March of 1971, the Air Force officially gave the two AX aircraft the following designations, A-9 for the Northrop prototype and A-10 for the Fairchild-Republic version. The first Fairchild prototype was finished during early 1972 and made its first flight at Edwards Air Force Base, California on 10 May 1972 with the second A-10 prototype flying later that July.

The A-10 and A-9 were extremely different in appearance. The A-9 design employed a more conventional approach with shoulder mounted wings, engines located neatly in the fuselage under the wings and a single vertical fin. The A-10, by comparison, was more radical looking. It had a new configuration with the combination of the high rear fuselage podded engines, straight wings and dual fins. On 18 January 1973, Fairchild-Republic was announced as the winner of the flyoff competition.

A major reason for picking Fairchild was that the A-10 prototype was more representative of a production aircraft and there would be less transition difficulty in bringing the aircraft into full scale production. Fairchild's gamble of asking for more money for their initial prototypes had paid off.

The best way to describe the A-10 design in non-technical terms is that it is really a "aircraft built around a gun". The gun was a 30MM Gatling gun designated the GAU-8A Avenger which was built by General Electric in their upstate New York plant. The Avenger gun can fire foot long 30MM shells made of spent uranium at a rate of 4,000

The prototype was loaded into a C-124 Globemaster II for the trip to Edwards AFB. At this time the aircraft was armed with a 20MM cannon, since the 30MM gun was not ready for installation. (Fairchild-Republic)

The second YA-10 prototype was completed two months after the first aircraft and it joined the first YA-10 at Edwards AFB in June of 1970. (Fairchild-Republic)

rounds a minute. The maximum load carried in the A-10 was 1,350 rounds, giving the aircraft thirty seconds of continuous fire, although it would be highly unlikely that any A-10 pilot would ever fire for more than a second or two. The high rate of fire was sufficient to destroy most armored targets. The large size of the gun forced an off-center location of the nose gear so that both would fit in the forward fuselage.

Besides the 30MM cannon, the A-10 could carry a wide variety of weapons under its wings, such as cluster bombs and the Maverick anti-armor missile. It also could carry the Pave Penny tracking system. There are many different weapons combinations that could be used, depending on the mission profile. These options gave the aircraft added flexibility and an advantage over other attack aircraft in the USAF inventory.

The aircraft has unique structural and aerodynamic features to maximize both survivability and maneuverability. The TF 34 turbofan engines built by General Electric were enclosed in nacelles that were extended above the wings, away from the lower fuselage. This feature was employed in the design primarily to lower the engines vulnerability to enemy ground fire as well as keeping them away from foreign object damage (FOD) and other debris during takeoff. The cockpit. is enclosed in a titanium armor "bathtub" to protect the pilot from enemy ground fire. The aircraft has triple redundancy for its flight control system, dual hydraulic lines, a backup manual control system in case of severe damage and self-sealing fuel tanks that do not explode when hit. The aircraft is advertised as being able to fly back home if it lost one engine, lost part of one wing and part of the tail section. The empennage section is a unique dual tail design which aided in the aircraft's stability and maneuverability as well as aiding in masking the infrared heat of the engine from detection.

The A-10 avionics include TACAN, radar, a Identification Friend or Foe (IFF) system and electronic countermeasures such as chaff and flares. It had a Heads Up Display (HUD) that was used for picking out and setting up targets for attack. The A-10 did not carry equipment for night attack missions and was considered a daytime attack aircraft. Therefore, in comparison to the other attack and fighter aircraft, it was much less complicated. The simplicity of its design did; however, improved its overall reliability and maintainability, as was later proven in field service.

In February of 1973, the Fiscal 1974 Defense Budget was released. It included 82 million dollars for the purchase of ten preproduction A-10As and 30 million dollars for long lead time components for the first A-10 production lot. However, before production was to get underway another political hurdle had to be overcome.

Development

YA-10

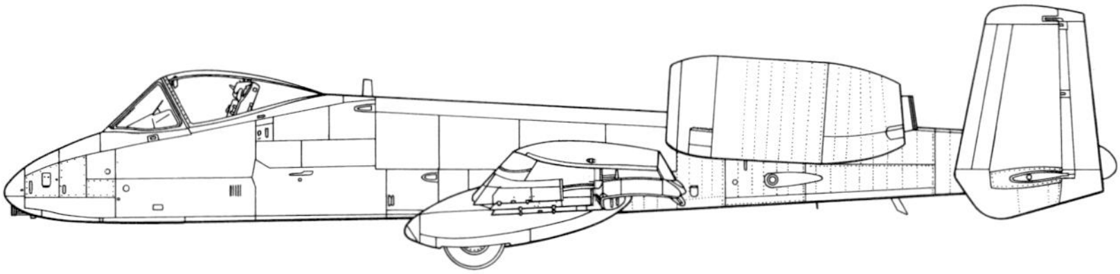

A-10A (Early)

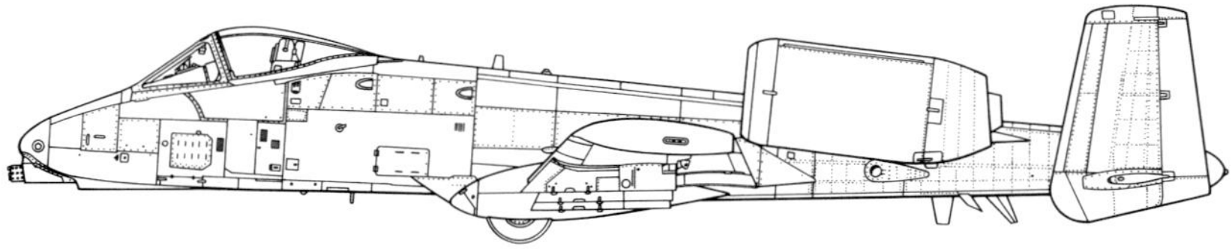

A-10A (Late)

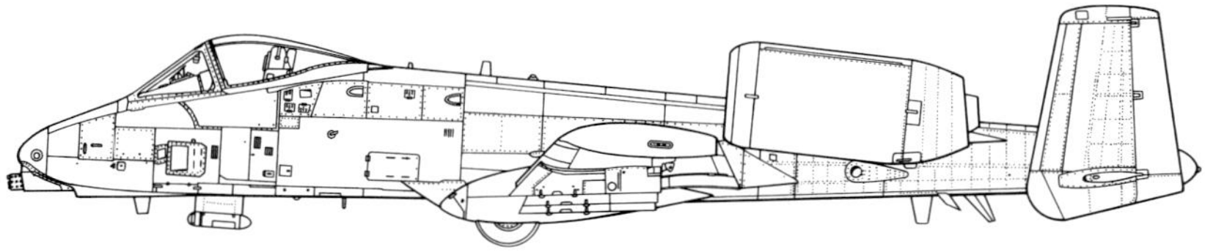

A-10A (N/AW)

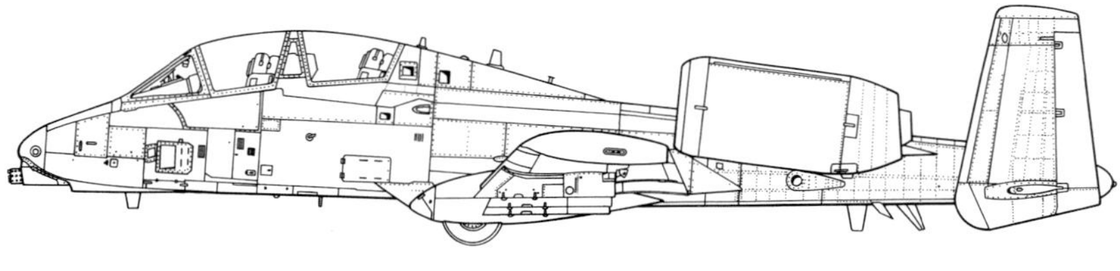

A-10 Firebomber (Proposed)

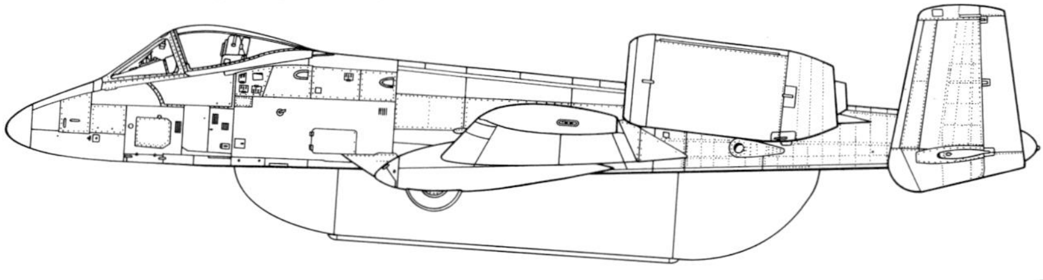

A-10A Thunderbolt II

Before full scale production of the A-10A could begin, a final political block had to be overcome. The congressional delegation from Texas was pushing the older A-7D Corsair aircraft that was built by Vought in Texas, as being able to meet the CAS mission requirements. The argument was that the A-7D was a proven aircraft and currently in production, and would therefore be cheaper to obtain in the numbers needed to meet the requirement than a new aircraft.

As a result of this political lobbying, the Senate Armed Services Committee withheld 30 million dollars originally earmarked for the long lead items for the first A-10 production lot. Additionally, both the House and the Senate mandated that another flyoff be conducted between the A-10 and the A-7D.

The second flyoff started 15 April 1974 at Fort Riley, Kansas where a data collection system existed for the recording of quantitative data from both aircraft. By May, it was decided that the A-10 was the better aircraft for the CAS mission, particularly in the area of target spotting in less than ideal conditions. Deputy Secretary of Defense William Clements would testify in front of Congress that the flyoff results were unanimous in favor of the A-10 and the program was allowed to resume with full expectations for production. Congress would approve a military appropriations bill that allocated 138 million dollars for the first twenty-five production aircraft with 20 million dollars restored from the earlier cut. The final obstacle was now removed and Fairchild was able to resume its new lease on life and go into production with the A-10.

With the last hurdle of the second flyoff over, long lead items were being ordered for the first batch of fifty-two aircraft that would follow the initial order for ten preproduction aircraft. This initial order included six DT&E (Development, Test and Evaluation) aircraft, and four production models that were initially assigned to Edwards Air Force Base. The A-10 production line would start with all six DT&E aircraft being built at the company's Farmingdale, Long Island plant. Each DT&E aircraft would be used for a different test or evaluation as follows: Aircraft #1, aerodynamic studies on loads and flutter (no gun installed). Aircraft # 2,weapons and systems testing. Aircraft # 3, weapons and system testing. Aircraft #4, performance testing (no gun installed). Aircraft #5, initial operational test and evaluation. Aircraft #6, climate testing (conducted at Eglin AFB, Florida). In addition to the six DT&E aircraft, there were two airframes built for stat-

The fin on the prototypes differed from the production A-10A in that it had a angled leading edge. Production A-10As changed to a rounded off leading edge. (Fairchild-Republic)

The first prototype YA-10 was joined in the test program by six DT&E (Development, Test and Evaluation) pre-production aircraft. Each aircraft had a different function in the program. At this point the prototype had been fitted with the 30MM cannon. (Fairchild-Republic)

ic and fatigue testing, with the second being tested in a separate test lab area in the Farmingdale plant.

In addition to the DT&E aircraft, the first four production aircraft (numbers 7 through 10) would be built entirely at the Farmingdale facility. After aircraft 10, it was decided to divide up the subassembly work between Farmingdale and the company's Hagerstown plant in Maryland, with final assembly and flight testing being conducted at Hagerstown because Fairchild no longer owned the adjacent Republic airport in Farmingdale. Scheduling flight test time would become difficult so it was decided that doing all flight testing in Hagerstown would alleviate this problem. The initial rate of production was one aircraft a month with a maximum rate of fourteen aircraft a month by 1980.

The A-10 used simple construction techniques that kept tooling costs down. Standard conical or flat shapes were used for skin surfaces which would keep the need for any elaborate sheet metal forming to a minimum. An example of this was the engine

This is the Titanium armor "bathtub" assembly that protects the cockpit area from ground fire. (Fairchild-Republic)

Fin Development

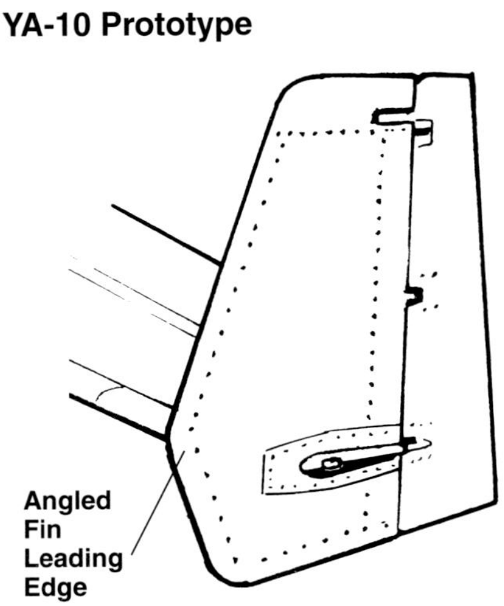

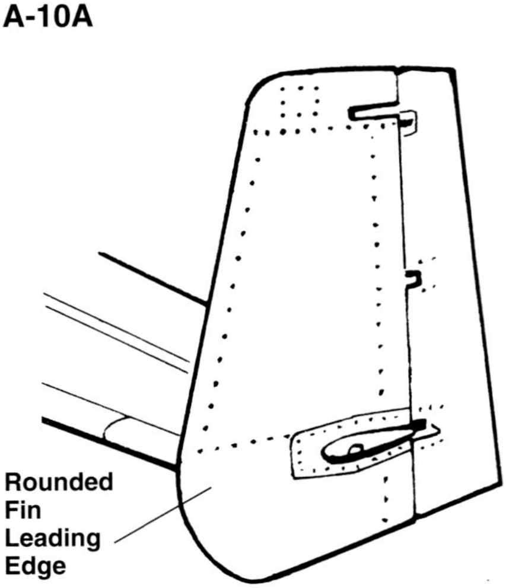

nacelles, which were a cylindrical shape in lieu of the more exotic teardrop shapes used by other military aircraft. The aircraft was unique in that it had a large number of interchangeable components between the left and right side of the airframe. Not only were the fins, rudders, main landing gears, wing panels, fuselage sections and pylons interchangeable but so were the engines. The A-10 was the first Air Force twin engined aircraft where the engines could be interchanged. The advantages was obvious.- fewer different parts cut down the documentation and simplified spares support.

The production A-10A differed little from the prototypes. One external difference was in the shape of the fin and rudder. Production A-10As had a rounded lower fin in place of the prototype's squared off fin. A fully loaded A-10A can reach a maximum

Painted in a Yellow-Green primer, these A-10As are undergoing final assembly on the Hagerstown assembly line. The next stop on the line will be the paint shop. (Fairchild-Republic)

An A-10A on the final assembly line at the Fairchild-Republic Hagerstown facility. At this point in the line the 30MM GAU-8 cannon has not yet been installed. (Fairchild-Republic)

speed of 450 knots or 518 miles per hour, well below supersonic range. Typical loiter speed of the aircraft in a combat profile was around 390 to 400 miles an hour. As based on the experiences of German Stuka pilots in the Second World War, slower speeds were more desirable in attacking armor targets. This slower speed became a sticking point for the Air Force, which was used to high speed aircraft, and this negative image

The first production A-10A was disassembled and placed on a transporter for loading into a C-5A at the Republic Airport in January of 1975 for its trip to Edwards AFB. Once reassembled at Edwards, the A-10A was fully operational. (Fairchild-Republic)

The second production A-10A, also known as the Number 2 DT&E aircraft, lifts off from the Fairchild-Republic facility for its delivery flight to Edwards AFB. This was the first A-10A to fly out of the plant and the first to conduct a cross-country flight. (Fairchild-Republic)

The Number 2 DT&E aircraft is prepared for a series of gun firing trials at Edwards AFB, California. The aircraft carried a Black 7 on the nose with a Red lightning bolt running through it. (Fairchild-Republic)

The A-10 is powered by a pair of General Electric TF34 turbofan engines that are very quiet in comparison to conventional jet engines. At 9,000 lbst, the engines provided all the power needed for the A-10 to carry out its mission. (Fairchild-Republic)

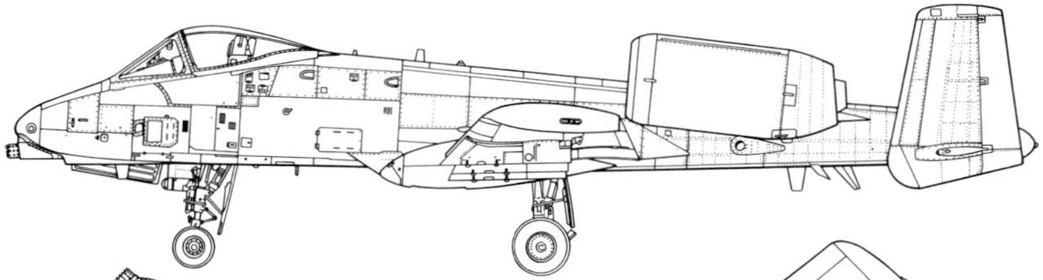

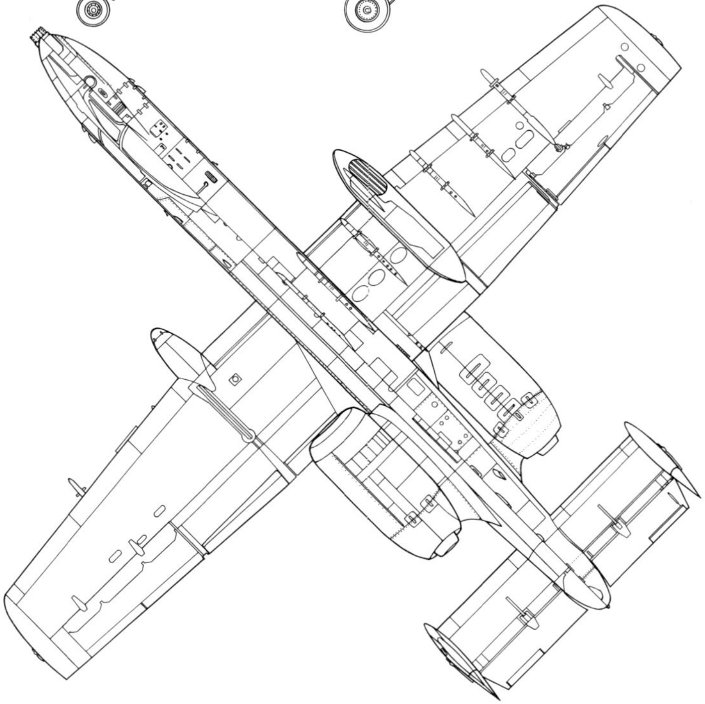

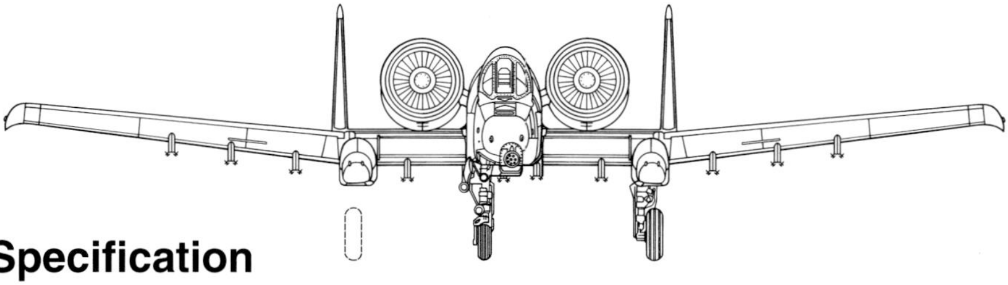

Specification

Fairchild-Republic A-10

Wingspan..............57 feet 6 inches (17.5 m)
Length...................53 feet 4 inches (16 m)
Height....................14 feet 8 inches (4.50 m)
Empty Weight....... 24,200 pounds (10,977 kg)
Maximum Weight..47,400 pounds (21,500 kg)
Powerplant............Two GE 9,000 lbst TF34-GE-100 turbofan engines.
Armament..............One 30MM Gau 8 Seven Barrel Gatling cannon, up to 16,000 pounds of underwing ordnance on ten stations..

Speed....................368 mph (592.2 kph)
Service Ceiling....34,400 feet (10,485 m)
Range...................2,160 miles 3,476 km)
Crew......................One

A pair of early production A-10As on the ramp at the Fairchild-Republic Hagerstown facility. The Hagerstown facility was used for test flights because of its more rural location and less crowded airspace. The aircraft are in the Ghost Gray camouflage used early in the A-10 program (Fairchild- Republic)

A ground crewman directs the pilot of an early production A-10A to taxi to the duty runway. The aircraft is configured with Multiple Ejector Racks (MERs) on the fuselage pylons. The two tone Ghost Gray camouflage scheme was designed to make it difficult to pick the aircraft out against the sky. (Fairchild-Republic)

The first operational A-10A unit was the 354th Tactical Fighter Wing at Myrtle Beach, South Carolina. This aircraft is painted in the European I camouflage scheme and carried a squadron badge painted on the fuselage behind the cockpit. (Ken Kubik)

of the A-10 would haunt it throughout the life of the program.

The aircraft's empty operating weight is 24,200 pounds and with the full compliment of weapons and fuel this weight increased to a maximum of 47,000 pounds. With four bombs, full 30MM ammunition load and 4,000 pounds of fuel, the aircraft could take off on an unimproved runway that was 1,900 feet long. At maximum takeoff weight, the runway distance required was 4,500 feet, far below that of most modern fighter aircraft. The aircraft is extremely quiet during takeoff in comparison to the roar of other jet fighters' afterburners. This would prove to be a very important feature in the battlefield. The A-10 has a combat loiter time of close to two hours ensuring that it could be over the battlefield and provide ground support for a long period. The aircraft also had the capability for in-flight refueling, giving the A-10 even longer ranges and loiter times. This would prove essential when the A-10 made the trans-

This A-10A Warthog of the 23rd Tactical Fighter Wing, based at England Air Force Base, Louisiana, carries the famous "Flying Tiger" sharksmouth marking used by the 23rd Fighter Group during the Second World War. The wing consists of the 74th, 75th and 76th Tactical Fighter Squadrons (TFS). The 74th and 76th TFSs saw action in Operation DESERT STORM. (Ken Kubik)

This A-10A carried a special camouflage scheme for the Joint Attack Weapon Systems (JAWS) test held in November of 1977, at Fort Hunter Ligget, California. The paint scheme was used for this series of exercises only and was not used operationally by any A-10 unit. (Fairchild-Republic)

Atlantic flight for deployment in Europe.

The first production A-10, Aircraft Number 7, flew in October of 1975 and was delivered to the Air Force the following month. Aircraft 7 through 10 were sent to Edwards AFB to join the ongoing test program.

The first aircraft to be delivered to an

Ejection Seats

A-10A (Early)
Excapac Seat

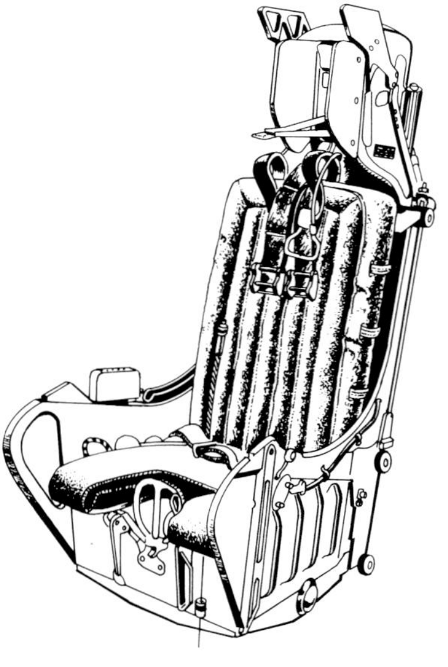

A-10A (Late) & OA-10
ACES II Seat

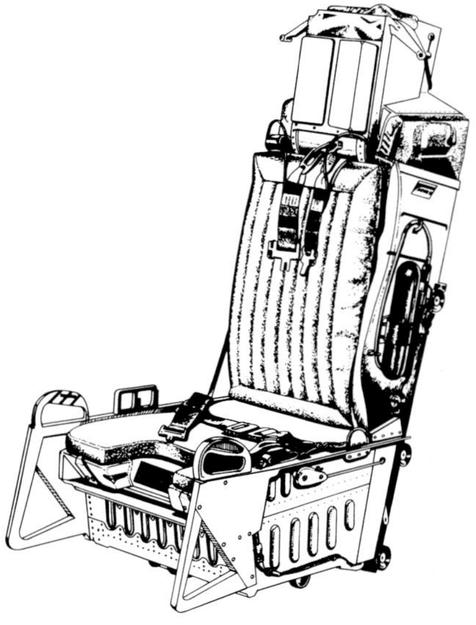

This early A-10 took part in a demonstration of the aircraft to the Imperial Iranian Air Force during May of 1975. Efforts to export the A-10 were hampered by U.S. restrictions on its spent Uranium ammunition, as well as the specialized nature of the aircraft. As a result, no A-10s were ever exported. (Fairchild-Republic)

operational base was Aircraft 11 which was taken on charge by the 333rd Tactical Fighter Training Squadron of the 364th Tactical Training Wing based Davis Monthan AFB in Tucson, Arizona.

Operations

On 3 April 1978, the century mark of the program was reached when Aircraft number 100 was delivered to the Air Force. The Air Force used the occasion to officially designate the A-10 as the Thunderbolt II, however, pilots had already coined their own name for the aircraft and that was — Warthog (because of its appearance). Other milestones for the A-10 took place during 1978 with the first combat ready wing being established in June, this was the 354th Tactical Fighter Wing at Myrtle Beach AFB, South Carolina. This conversion process took five months less than originally planned. In December, an A-10 from the 355th Tactical Fighter Wing at Davis Monthan AFB, Arizona, became the first A-10 to go over the 1,000 hour mark. The first A-10 delivered to the Air National Guard reached the 174th TFW based at Martin Air Force Base, Baltimore, Maryland during September of 1979. This was the beginning of a program to equip four more ANG groups with A-10s over the next five years.

Europe received its first A-10 in January of 1979 when part of the 81st Tactical Fighter Wing arrived at RAF Bentwaters, Suffolk, England. This was the beginning of the USAF's anti-armor commitment to NATO. NATO was facing a disadvantage of tank strength against the Warsaw Pact of almost three to one and the A-10 was there to counter this ratio. The Warthogs that would be assigned to Bentwaters would frequently deploy to several forward operating bases in West Germany. In all, the designated strength of the 81st TFW would be six squadrons totaling 108 aircraft by 1980 and the A-10 would be a well-known sight on European bases. Shortly after the A-10 was deployed to Europe, it was determined that the pilot workload was very high due to the European terrain and that some additional navigational aids would be required. The change that resulted was the addition of an Inertial Navigation System (INS), which was retrofitted throughout the entire A-10 fleet.

As more and more production A-10s were being deployed into the field, certain problems with the design became noticeable. One of them was the problem of engine stallout occurring during the firing of the gun and a number of incidents had occurred. The earliest occurrence of the problem was in June of 1978 when A-10 Number 6 had both engines stall during testing of the 30MM ammunition propellant at Edwards AFB. The problem was caused by the high concentration of gun gas particles that would accumulate and foul the engines during gun firing. A joint team of Fairchild Republic engineers and Air Force personnel tackled the problem and were able to develop effective corrective action to both the gun and aircraft design by 1981.

The A-10 was subjected to a series of operational tests, beginning in 1977, that were designed to test its ability to fly multiple sorties in a single day using different scenarios. These tests were as follows: At Gila Bend AFB in Arizona during February of 1977, two A-10As flew a combined total of 34 sorties in eleven continuous hours. This was one of the earliest exercises that tested the aircraft's high sortie rate capability. The Joint Attack Weapon Systems (JAWS) test was held in November of 1977, at Fort Hunter Ligget in California. These tests were designed to see how well the A-10 worked with the Army's AH-1 Cobra helicopter. The scenario would have the A-10s concentrating on conventional ground targets, such as tanks, while the Cobras would concentrate on attacking air defense systems. The tests would be conducted in as realistic a wartime environment as possible although no live ammunition was used (blanks were fired). The conclusion drawn was that by having the A-10 and the Cobra working together, the kill ratios went up three to four times over when each operated separately. In January of 1978, the first Operational Readiness Inspection (ORE) was conducted by the 356th TFS at the Savannah, Georgia Air National Guard base in Travis Field. A squadron of twenty-four Warthogs flew 319 sorties in four days, yielding an average sortie rate of three per day per aircraft. In addition, target runs were conducted at nearby Fort Stewart and the A-10s expended over 25,000 rounds of 30MM ammunition and 420 Mk 282 training bombs. During a validation test at Shaw AFB in South Carolina from 17-24 April 1978, one squadron of eighteen A-10s few 324 sorties in three days for a sortie rate of six per aircraft per day. During the test, one A-10 flew twenty-two consecutive sorties without a maintanance problem. All aircraft were fully mission capable at the conclusion of the exercises. At Operation CORONET FILLEY held in March of 1979 in Suwon, South Korea, a squadron of A-10s achieved a sortie rate of five per aircraft per day with a peak of seven being reached. In April of 1981 at RAF Bentwaters, a one day surge effort was conducted by the 81st TFW called

Ground crewmen prepare to load 30MM ammunition into the ammunition canister of an A-10A of the Massachussets Air National Guard. The automatic loader takes ammunition from the bin on the trailer and loads it into the internal ammunition canister of the GAU-8 cannon. (Ken Kubik)

An Air National Guard A-10 takes on fuel from a KC-135 of the 170th Air Refueling Group. (Rick Llinares - Flight Line Photography)

PORKER 500. A fleet of eighty-nine A-10s flew 579 hours while flying 533 sorties in fourteen hours yielding a one day sortie rate of almost six per aircraft per day. Several other Operational Readiness Inspections would be held in the early 1980s. At England AFB, the 76th TFS achieved a one day sortie. rate of six by flying 117 sorties by twenty-four aircraft.

The success of the A-10 Warthog in these exercises would draw many favorable comments from top level officials. Lieutenant General Kelly Burke, the Deputy Chief of Staff for USAF Research, Development and Acquisition testified at the Military Posture hearings held by the House of Representatives Armed Service Committee in March of 1980. He said, "We get a higher sortie rate from the A-10 than any of our aircraft. It is capable of about six sorties per day and had the lowest operating cost of any of our first line fighters."

By the early 1980's the A-10 would be primarily deployed at five Air Force bases and four Air National Guard bases.

The 57th Fighter Weapons Wing was located at Nellis AFB Las Vegas, Nevada. The 355th Tactical Training Wing was at Davis Monthan AFB, Tucson, Arizona. The 354th Tactical Fighter Wing was at Myrtle Beach AFB, Myrtle Beach, South Carolina. The 23rd Tactical Fighter Wing was located at England AFB, Alexandria, Louisiana and the 81st Tactical Fighter Wing was at RAF Bentwaters, Woodbridge, Great Britain

National Guard units included the 174th TFW at Hancock AFB Syracuse, New York. The 103rd TFGat Bradley AFB,Winsdor Locks, Connecticut, the 104th TFG based at Barnes AFB, Westfield, Massachussetts and the 175th TFG at Martin AFB, Baltimore, Maryland

Subsequent years would bring many changes and reassignments of A-10s to different Air Force and Air National Guard bases, both at home and overseas.

An A-10A in the European I camouflage shares the ramp at Langley Air Force Base, Virginia with its ancestor, the Republic F-105 Thunderchief. (Fairchild-Republic)

A-10A N/AW

There was hope since the beginning of the A-10 program that an enhanced variant of the aircraft could be developed for the Air Force. This hope was based on the original Air Force A-10 System Specification that was written in 1972 and stated that "the vehicle design shall allow for ease of growth to a two-place version for training (with combat capability) and night/adverse weather attack." During 1978, the DOD made funds available for development of a Night/Adverse Weather (N/AW) variant of the A-10.

The N/AW development effort was jointly funded by the Defense Department and Fairchild-Republic (five million and two million dollars respectively). As part of this effort, Fairchild leased the first DT&E A-10 aircraft from the Air Force for the purpose of modifying it into an two seat variant designated the N/AW evaluator. As Fairchild had allowed for expansion in the original design, the amount of rework to be performed on the leased aircraft would not be drastic.

The N/AW version was built primarily as a reaction to the fact that Soviet forces in Europe devote about forty percent of their training to night operations. Current A-10s could operate at night using illumination flares, but that activity would be nullified by reduced visibility. As a result, a. requirement existed for evaluating a version that could fly in all types of weather.

The rework began in April of 1978 at the Farmingdale plant and took over thirteen months to complete. The N/AW version was 2,000 pounds heavier than a conventional A-10 with the addition of a second cockpit station for the Weapons System Officer (WSO). This extra station included a duplicate of the forward cockpit except for the HUD, controls and the titanium bathtub. Flight control systems would be duplicated with the addition of a second yaw stick.

New avionics added to the N/AW evaluator were a multimode radar and a Forward Looking Infrared (FLIR). The multimode radar had modes for target indication, ground mapping, terrain tracking and target detection. The threat detector function could detect radar signals from a surface-to-air missile battery or a radar directed anti-aircraft gun. The FLIR presented a realistic image of the terrain on the Heads up Display and could be used for target identification for the 30MM gun, INS updating and as a secondary terrain avoidance monitor to the multimode radar.

Besides the second cockpit, the N/AW differed from the A-10A in that the fin and rud-

The Night/All Weather A-10 two seat prototype rests in a hangar at Edwards Air Force Base, California during the evaluation of the aircraft. The aircraft has a Owl holding an umbrella painted on the nose. (Fairchild-Republic)

Each nacelle cover on the A-10A N/AW prototype had a eye painted on it. The aircraft was evaluated by the Air Force during May of 1979. Although the aircraft performed well, it was decided that A-10As equipped with LANTERN would be capable of performing the same mission. (Fairchild-Republic)

der was modified. The N/AW fin and rudder were enlarged to improve laterial stability and control.

The aircraft was delivered to Edwards AFB for Air Force flight testing, which began on 4 May 1979. The initial flights were devoted to air worthiness checks in the area of control handling from both cockpits. Also, new equipment such as the low altitude warning sensors was checked out in the

Fuselage Development

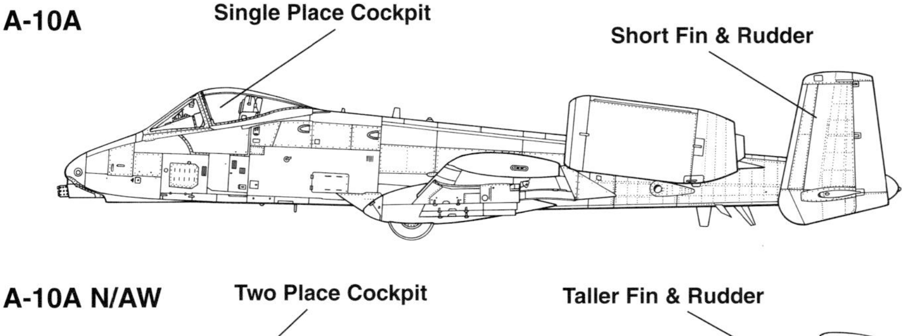

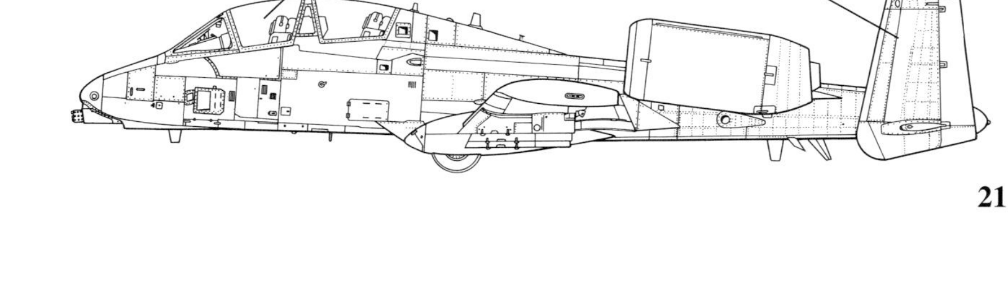

The Night/All Weather A-10 did part of its evaluation at Galilero Hills Air Force Base, California during August of 1979. The aircraft was capable of carrying the same armament as the single seat A-10, including the 30MM cannon. (Fairchild-Republic)

various types of terrain and structures on the ground. After the initial flights, tactical evaluations were carried out that included low altitude flying, target detection and gun attacks. The prime objective of the Air Force with the N/AW evaluator was to see if the additional equipment could be handled by one pilot. This could lead into enhanced single-seat A-10s being developed by retrofitting the A-10 fleet. Fairchild was coming from a different perspective as it felt that the N/AW function was a two-man job.

Cost estimates for converting an A-10 to the two seat configuration were $500,000 for the basic structural work and another million dollars for the additional

Canopy Development

A-10A

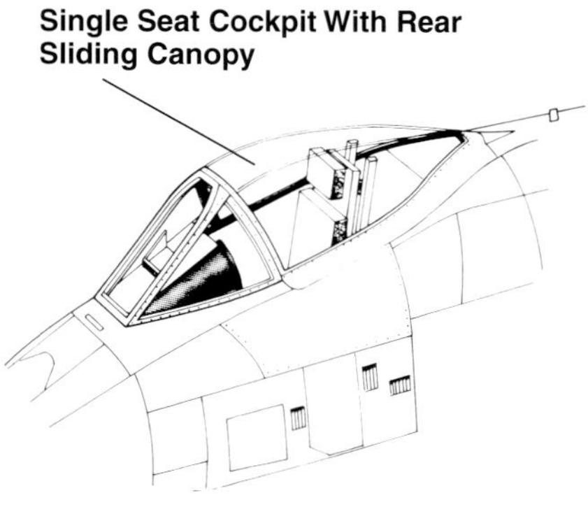

A-10A N/AW

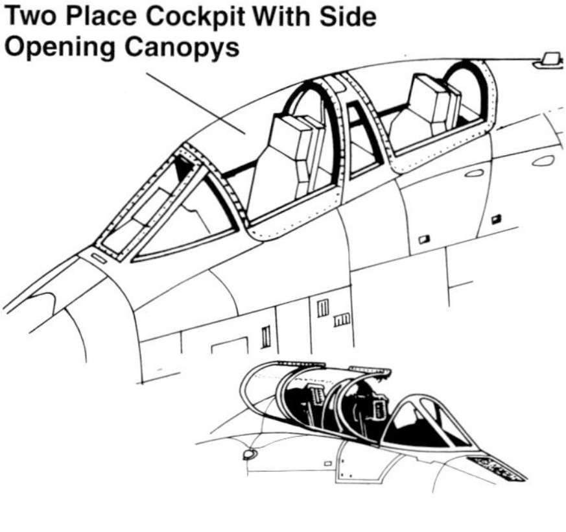

The N/AW A-10 conducts an evaluation flight near Edwards Air Force Base, California during the Summer of 1979. This was the only two seat A-10 built since production of the A-10B trainer was cancelled by congress during 1983. (Fairchild-Republic)

Night/Adverse Weather equipment. The Air Force; however, was looking into the possibility of having single seat A-10s converted into N/AW aircraft. In the event, the LANTERN (Low Altitude Night Time Infrared Navigation) system was proposed for the A-10 ending the need for the N/AW specialized aircraft. as the LANTERN enhanced pilot capability for night time flying. Throughout the next decade, the LANTERN proposal would go through several design alterations and several nomenclature changes with the end result that no enhanced system was put into the A-10 before the end of production,

There was also a proposal for a two-seat trainer when the Air Force asked for trade studies on such an aircraft. This was different from the N/AW evaluator as the second seat would be added for training purposes only and no advanced electronics would be added to this version which was designated as the A-l0B. Data collected from flight testing of the N/AW evaluator provided the

Fin & Rudder Development

A-10A

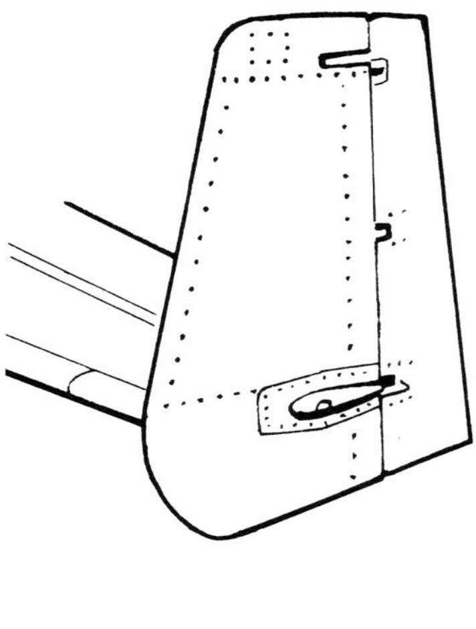

A-10A N/AW

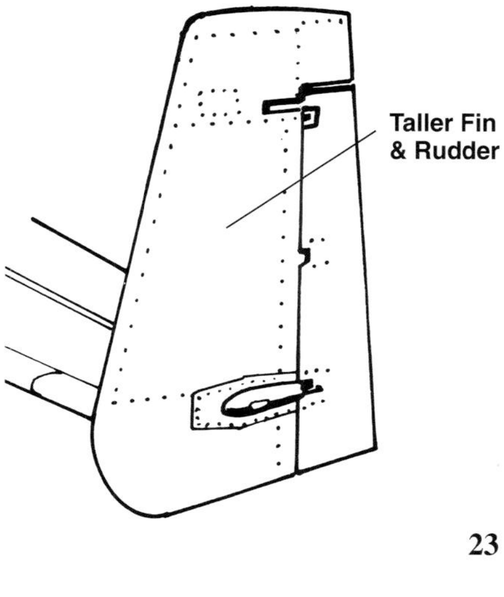

Air Force with enough information to make a decision. The Air Force requested that twenty A-10B aircraft be tacked on to the original order of 713 aircraft. If additional A-10Bs were needed, then existing A-10As would be converted.

The proposed A-10B version was cut by congress during 1983 who felt, along with several Air Force officials, that the A-10A was already simple enough to fly and that a trainer version was not needed. The final count for A-10 production was 713 aircraft. The only two seat version for the A-10 program was the N/AW aircraft which still exists today, but only as a museum piece at Edwards AFB.

The inability of Fairchild-Republic to obtain an extension to the existing A-10 contract, along with the Air Force's cancellation of the company's other prime program, the controversial T-46A trainer program, forced it to close during early 1987. The rights of the A-10 program, along with 116 engineers were obtained by Grumman Aerospace late in 1987.

In the late 1980s, there was a discussion about transferring A-10s to the Army. Instead, a slightly modified version for reconnaissance, designated the OA-10, was developed. This variant required minimal modification to existing A-10s with the external difference being what was carried under the wings. Instead of bombs and missiles, the OA-10 carried White phosphorus rockets for marking targets for other aircraft to destroy. The OA-10 would still carry a full load of ammunition for the 30MM cannon for self defense. There were two groups of A-10s that were converted to OA-10 standards and these were stationed at Davis-Monthan AFB in Tucson, Arizona.

The prototype Night/All Weather A-10 still exists. The aircraft is on display at Edwards Air Force Base, California as part of the base museum. (Fairchild-Republic)

Variation of the Warthog nose art used on aircraft of the 917th Tactical Fighter Wing at Barksdale AFB, Louisiana.

45th TFS

This A-10A of the 45th Tactical Fighter Squadron carried D-Day Invasion stripes during May of 1994 as the unit prepared to take part in special D-Day activities marking the 50th anniversary of the invasion.

This was an experimental desert scheme carried on A-10As of the 917th TFW at Barksdale AFB. The scheme was not adopted for service use.

This A-10A of the 23rd TFW is camouflaged in Dark and Light Ghost Gray and carried a sharkmouth in Red, White and Black. The checkerboard fin tip was Black and White.

Tactical Air Command

23rd TFW

This Gray mottle early production A-10A was assigned to the Aeronautical Systems Command at Edwards AFB during 1977.

Aeronautical Systems Command

The first production A-10A was retained for test work and carried an instrument probe on the nose. The overall Gunship Gray aircraft was based at Edwards AFB during mid-1975.

57th TTW

This A-10A of the 57th TTW carried a one of a kind camouflage known as the JAWS scheme during 1978. The scheme was a wrap-around camouflage designed to confuse ground gunners of what direction the A-10 was turning.

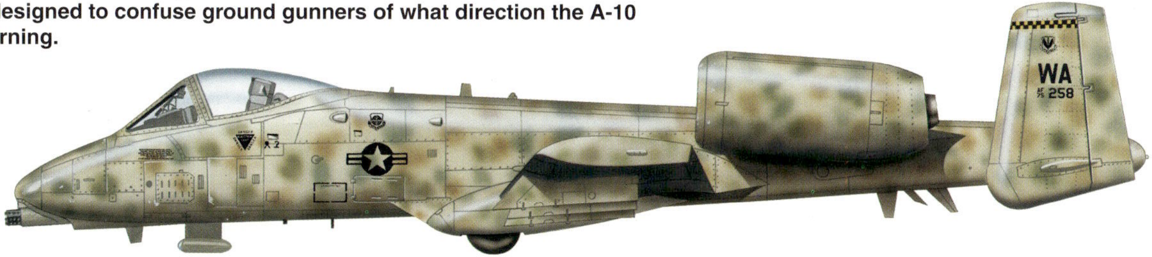

Tactical Air Command

DESERT STORM

With the development of impending hostilities over the takeover of Kuwait by Iraq in August of 1990, the United States received permission from Saudi Arabia to deploy their forces on Saudi bases. The Iraqi army, at that time, had the fourth largest army in the world, consisting of over 4,000 tanks and 4,000 artillery pieces. Logically, the A-10 should have been high on the list of assets to be deployed there in order to counter the Iraqi armored threat, but there was initial hesitation from upper echelon Air Force officials to do so, since they favored higher speed fighters such as the F-16. Due to the direct intervention of the commander of the Coalition forces, United States Army General Schwarzkopf, this initial decision was overturned and several squadrons of A-10s were deployed to the Gulf region. As an army man, the General was well aware of the A-10's capabilities, more so than most officials of the Air Force.

A sizable A-10 force was assembled at King Fahd International Airport, comprising both A-10s and the reconnaissance OA-10s. The 354th Tactical Fighter Wing (TFW) out of Myrtle Beach AFB deployed the 353rd and 355th Tactical Fighter Squadrons (TFS) with a total of fifty-three A-10s. The 23rd TFW from England AFB sent the 74th and 76th TFS with forty-eight A-10s. The l0th TFW deployed the 511th TFS from RAF Alconbury with eighteen A-10s. The 926th Tactical Fighter Group sent eighteen A-10s of the 705th TFS and the 602nd Tactical Air Control Wing deployed fifteen OA-10As from Davis-Monthan AFB with the 23rd TASS. The 152 A-10 aircraft that were deployed to Saudi Arabia represented eight percent of all United States military aircraft (not counting helicopters) that were deployed to the Gulf.

After several tense months, war broke out on 16 January 1991, and the A-10s were committed to combat for the first time in its twenty year life. The DESERT STORM operation presented several new opportunities for the Warthog that had not been foreseen by the military experts prior to the war. It would surprise the experts with the ease that it took on these new roles along with its predetermined role as tank killer.

During the early part of the war, after Iraq launched numerous Scud-B missiles at

This A-10 of the 23rd Fighter Wing was parked on the ramp at King Fahd Airport armed with Cluster Bomb Units (CBUs), four Maverick missiles, ECM pods and a twin AIM-9 Sidewinder missile rail. Reportedly, Iraqi soldiers nicknamed the A-10 "the circling buzzard." (SSGT Robert Pease)

Dual Sidewinder Mount

A-10A & OA-10A

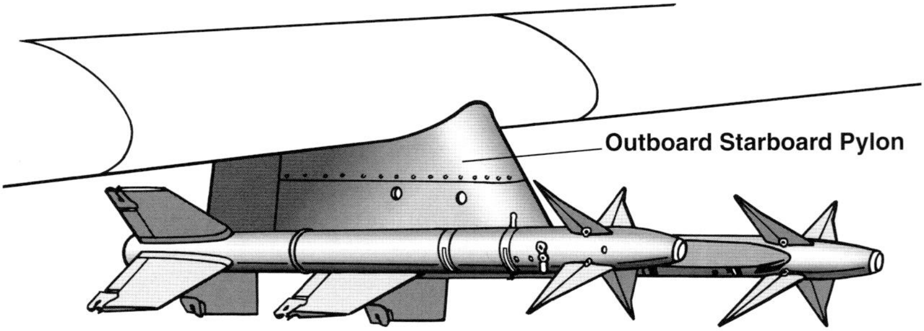

Saudi Arabia and Israel, the A-10 would be pressed into service as a Scud hunter. The A-10 Warthog became the aircraft of choice to do this job because it could fly closer to the ground than any other attack aircraft as well as being a long-duration aircraft that could loiter over Iraqi territory for several hours. Teams of A-10s and OA-10s would orbit, waiting for a signal from the overhead surveillance aircraft to look for newly targeted Scud-B missile launches. The pilots would trace the missile flight path back to the area where the missile had been fired and then use their visual skills to find the launcher and use whatever ordnance that they had onboard to kill the target. Scud hunting was conducted from the forward operating base at Al Jouf. The tough task of finding the

A female groundcrew member removes the safety pins from a pair of AIM-9 Sidewinder air-to-air missiles mounted on the starboard outboard pylon of an A-10. These missiles were carried for self defense against Iraqi aircraft, although none were ever fired against Iraqi air targets during the war. Both A-10 air-to-air kills were gained using the cannon. (USAF)

This was the first A-10 to ever fly a combat mission returns to base after a sortie against Iraqi targets on 16 January 1992, the first day of Operation DESERT STORM. The aircraft still carried its AIM-9 missiles. (Fred Schlenker III)

disguised mobile launchers was described as, "trying to find a semi-trailer in Los Angeles," remarked Captain Colaw, the Public Information Officer of the 354th TFW that was one of the Wings employed for Scud hunting. The A-10 would record

This A-10 was flown by Captain Swain when he shot down an Iraqi helicopter with his 30MM GAU-8. The kill was recorded on the side of the fuselage in the form of a small Iraqi flag. The placard ACES II on the boarding ladder door indicates that this A-10 was equipped with an ACES II ejection seat rather than the earlier Escapac seat. (Fred Schlenker III)

Perhaps one of the most publicized incidents of the Gulf War concerned this A-10, flown by Captain Paul Johnson. The aircraft was hit by a surface-to-air missile which blew a twenty foot hole in the wing. Despite this damage, Captain Johnson was able to fly the aircraft back to base and make a safe landing. He was later to be awarded the Air Force Cross for this action and for an earlier "Sandy" rescue mission in southern Iraq. (Fred Schlenker III)

Maintenance personnel study the damage to Captain Johnson's A-10. In addition to the wing, the starboard engine was damaged as was the landing gear housing. The engine was replaced and the wing was eventually repaired, with the aircraft being returned to full mission ready status. It returned to combat in DESERT STORM. (USAF)

over fifty confirmed Scud missile launcher kills in this war.

From the outset of the war, the A-10 was thrust immediately into attacking fixed targets such as artillery pieces, airfields, bunkers and military command posts. The A-10 pilots would use a clever tactic on their attacks on Iraqi artillery. The A-10s would fly at 12,000 feet over enemy territory deliberately drawing fire from Iraqi AAA batteries. The A-10s; however, would be out of range for these AAA guns and now the A-

A maintenance crewman makes a sheet metal patch over bullet holes in this battle damaged A-10. Most damage was repairable in the field. (USAF)

A-10A Weapons Pylons

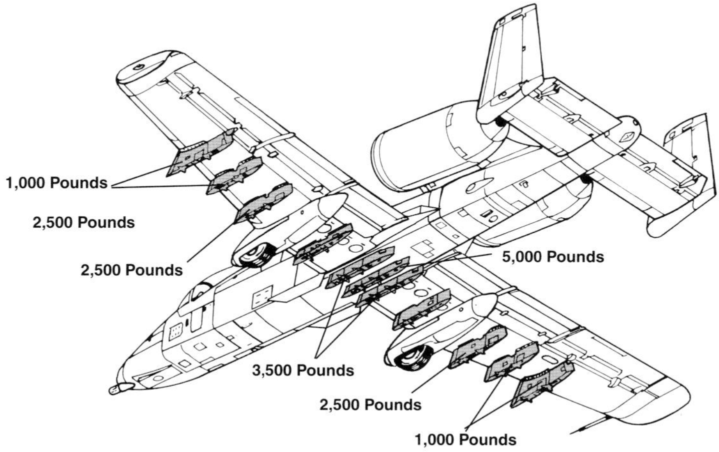

10 pilots would know exactly where the guns were and would attack them. Pilots would use both the Maverick missile and the 30MM gun equally in these attacks. All told, the A-10s were estimated to have destroyed about one half of the Iraqi artillery during the war.

On the afternoon of 21 January, two A-10 pilots, Captain Paul Johnson and Captain Randy Goff, of the 354th,were part of a dramatic rescue of a downed F-14 airman in southern Iraq. The rescue mission took over

This A-10A, flown by the wing commander of the 23rd TFW, returned to base despite severe damage to the elevators, fin, and rudders. The built-in survival features of the A-10 were proven over and over during the Gulf War. (USAF)

A-10s of the 926th Tactical Fighter Group, line up next to an ammunition loading area to take on weapons prior to a Gulf War mission. These aircraft are loaded with Maverick missiles and CBUs. (Fred Schlenker III)

eight hours and each Warthog had to be refueled in the air four times during this mission. The A-10s were able to successfully locate the airman and provided cover until a rescue helicopter arrived. An Iraqi truck appeared on the scene and was quickly destroyed by the A-10s. The A-10 would continue to be a major part of "Sandy" or rescue duty throughout the remainder of the war.

DESERT STORM was the debut of the OA-10 forward observer version. This variant was used in the target identification and marking role. Two separate OA-10 groups, comprising, fifteen aircraft from the 602nd Tactical Air Control Wing, which was a part of the 353rd Tactical Training Wing would provide the marking for over 3,000 targets during the war. During a reconnaissance mission, OA-10 pilots would be assigned a specific grid box drawn on the map of Kuwait that encompassed several hundred square miles, along with a list of potential targets to verify and then mark with the White phosphorus rockets. Each OA-10 forward air controller team would have pilots, air liaison officers (ALOs) and ground controllers that worked closely with the Army to find and mark each target. Once the targets were marked, attack aircraft such as A-10s, F-16s, A-6s and F-18s would be called in fifteen minutes later to attack the marked targets. On a number of occasions, OA-10s would also attack targets with their 30MM cannon.

On 6 February Captain Bob Swain, a reservist flying for the 926th TFG, recorded the first recorded A-10 air-to-air kill when he shot down an Iraqi helicopter with his cannon. This was repeated on 15 February when Captain Todd Scheeny of the 511th TFS shot down an Mi-8 with his cannon. On the same day as Swain's kill, another Warthog was severely hit and the pilot, Captain Paul Johnson of the 354th TFW (who had been involved in the dramatic rescue of a downed pilot two weeks previously) struggled to bring his damaged A-10 back to base. He was flying his first sortie since the rescue and during this particular mission , an attack of a SAM missile battery, Johnson's A-10 was the last to leave the target area and was hit by a shoulder launched SAM missile. The missile entered the underside of the right wing at the leading edge and left a gaping hole of over twenty feet stretched across the wing and the right main landing gear housing was blown away. Johnson was going to eject when he reached the Saudi border, but after jettisoning his remaining ordnance, he changed his mind when the plane picked up speed and decided to risk flying the aircraft to home base. He was able to successfully land the aircraft despite damage to the hydraulic lines and a blown out tire. He was awarded the Air Force

An engine technician repairs an oil leak on the port engine of an A-10 that was damaged by enemy ground fire. The tail pipe of the A-10 was slanted upward to help shield the exhaust from the ground (and the seeker heads of shoulder fired IR guided missiles). (Fred Schlenker III)

Cross for his courage in action for both this mission and the previous rescue mission.

The war showed how the A-10 could take hits and still survive. Bullets were seen bouncing off the titanium bathtub that protected the pilot. An A-10 lost much of its right rudder and elevator and still made it back. Another lost all flight controls in the tail section and was able to land safely with the pilot using engine and aileron controls only. An A-10 pilot, Captain Rich Biley, sustained major damage to the plane's tail section and was able to fly back to base for an emergency landing at a forward operating base in Saudi Arabia. Even though the A-10 was destroyed during the crash landing, Captain Biley was able to walk away from the wreck. The Warthog had proven to be a tough and efficient killer.

The Warthog was always thought of as a tank killer and this was the ideal war to prove this fact. The Soviet-built T-55, T-62 and T-72 tanks that comprised the Iraqi army were the targets that the A-10 was designed to take on when it was deployed in Europe. In the early part of the war; however, many of these tanks were camouflaged and buried in the sand and innovative tactics had to be developed to find them.

One of these was to fly a pair of A-10s at night, with one plane having all instrumentation off except for the infrared imaging system used with the Maverick missile, while the other would have full instrumentation and thus being the "eyes" for the pair. As metal cools off at a slower rate than the surrounding sand at night, the tanks would show up as a "bump" on the screen. The "blind" A-10 would then launch a Maverick missile at the target, usually with a direct hit. The 355th and 74th TFS were the two squadrons tasked with night hawk operations during the war.

When the Iraqi Army took the offensive at the border town at Khaji, the A-10 was called in to decimate the column of armored

This A-10 racked up quite a tally of Iraqi material. It carries kill marking for eight tanks, four armored cars, seven guns, four Scud missile launchers, three radars and eight trucks. (USAF)

vehicles. A-10 pilots employed a tactic that would become its trademark. On the first pass, they would attack the front and rear vehicles of the columns, effectively pinning the entire column for repeated attacks. When the coalition ground offensive began on 23 February, A-10s were sent to the Kuwait area to destroy the valves that moved the oil into the network of Iraqi defensive trenches. This phase of the war allowed many opportunities for the A-10 as Iraqi tanks were now in the open. On 25 February, two A-10 pilots, Captain Eric Salomonson and Lieutenant John Marks of the 23rd TFS, destroyed twenty-three tanks and damaged ten others in three separate

This A-10 assigned to Major General Link carried an impressive scoreboard of four radars, one Scud launcher, twelve guns, fourteen tanks, eight armored cars/armored personnel carriers, and eleven trucks. (Anthony Abbott)

An A-10 of the 355th Tactical Fighter Squadron on the ramp at Myrtle Beach Air Force Base, South Carolina upon the unit's homecoming in March of 1991. (Fred Schlenker III)

mission on a single day. The A-10 was making a visible impression on the Iraqi army as the appearance of the Warthog would cause many of them to abandon their tanks prior to the A-10 pilots making their first pass. The Iraqi ,left their positions in Kuwait and retreated toward Iraq on the six lane highway that connected Kuwait City and Basra. The columns of vehicles would fall prey to Navy A-6s, F-16s, B-52s, helicopters and A-10s with the end result being called the "highway of death". At the same time, A-10s were supporting the attack on Iraqi Republican Guard positions in southern Iraq. These missions continued until a cease fire was declared on 28 February.

Gulf Wrap-up

A Washington Post article written in March by columnist Jack Anderson referred to the performance of the A-10 Warthog as "The Hero that Almost Missed the War", referring the Air Force's initial's resistance to deploying the aircraft in the Kuwaiti theater. The A-10's performance helped shorten the war thanks to the high volume of Iraqi war material it destroyed in just forty-two days. The following kills were con-

Aircraft Number 654 led the 355th TFS in kills with one radar site, two Scuds, fourteen guns, six tanks, fifteen armored cars/armored personnel carriers and ten trucks. (Fred Schlenker III)

This aircraft has kill markings on the fuselage side in White, but lacks the written number total for each. The unit commander requested that the totals be removed from the aircraft prior to homecoming at Myrtle Beach AFB, South Carolina. (Fred Schlenker III)

firmed by the Air Force (as reported by the 23rd TFW's Fact Sheet of May 1991): 987 tanks, 926 artillery pieces, 500 Armored Personnel Carriers (APCs), 1,106 trucks, 112 military structures, 96 radar installations, 72 bunkers, 51 SCUD missile launchers, 50 anti-aircraft artillery batteries, 28 command posts, 11 FROG missiles, 9 SAM missile sites, 8 fuel tanks, 12 aircraft (on ground) and 2 helicopters (airborne).

United States Army estimates are much higher than the confirmed kill list, crediting the A-10 with between 25 and 50 percent of Iraq's 4,000 tanks, more than 50 percent of the 4,000 artillery pieces and more than 30 percent of Iraqi armored personnel carriers. It is probable that the true number that would be credited to the A-10 will never be known for sure, since there were also several hundred tanks damaged by A-10s.

The A-10 Warthogs flew a total of 8,500 sorties, averaging over two hours per mission. The A-10 sortie total accounted for over seven percent of the 109,876 total sorties flown with the aircraft amassing over 19,000 flying hours during the war period. The Warthogs flew more than one mission per day per plane and this was reflected in the Mission Capable rate of 96 percent, which exceeded the Air Force average of 92 percent for DESERT STORM.

There were a total of seventeen A-10s severely damaged and six aircraft destroyed. There were no Warthog losses until 2 February, when ground target attacks intensified in preparation for the ground war. Several of the damaged Warthogs had literally hundreds of bullet holes in the plane, yet the aircraft was able to return home. Of the six aircraft that were downed, two pilots was killed, another walked away, and three others ejected safely, suffering minor injuries. Captain Steve Phyllis went down with his aircraft while, Lieutenant Pat Olson, died trying to land his damaged OA-10.

The main knock against the A-10 prior to the war was that it was very slow and highly visible. While this is considered a handicap for an aircraft in the age of stealth technolo-

A number of A-10s came home from DESERT STORM with nose art, such as *Desert Belle*, BROTHERS IN ARMS, *Have Gun Will Travel* and LAKANUKI of the 926th TFS, most did not keep the nose art for long after returning home. (Anthony Abbott)

gy, it actually served as an advantage for the A-10 in its role as a terror weapon for the Coalition. It would become the most well known aircraft to the Iraqi ground forces, who quickly learned to fear the appearance of the Warthog. Iraqi POWs told interrogators they gave the A-10 the nickname, "circling buzzard." Despite the lack of stealth, the Iraqis had difficulty in spotting the A-10 until it was too late and the attack had begun. This was because the A-10's turbofan engines were quiet, especially in comparison to other Air Force aircraft and other noises that occur in the battlefield. It was estimated that the A-10 could not be heard on the battlefield for better than 95 percent of the time.

The A-10 was praised by many officers. General Merrill McPeak, the Air Force Chief of Staff said in early February (in reference to the original plans to retire the A-10), "We're going to keep the A-10 in the inventory as far as the eye can see." An army infantry officer said his troops loved the Warthog, adding, "It comes in and smashes tanks and armored vehicles. It's the A-10's day in the sun." Another Army officer said, "We would be in serious trouble if they hadn't come. They are the major weapon between us and the Iraqis." Most of all, the pilots appreciated how well the plane performed and survived. Even Air Force General Horner admitted that he was wrong in opposing the deployment of the A-10 to Saudi Arabia, "I take back all the bad things that I've ever said about the A-10s. I love them. They're saving our asses."

The statements from captured Iraqi officers on the A-10 were even more compelling. One Iraqi captain said, "The single most recognizable, and feared aircraft at low level was the A-10 Thunderbolt II. This dark-colored jet was deadly accurate, rarely missing its target. It conducted bombing raids three or four times a day and was a seemingly ubiquitous threat. Although the actual bomb run was terrifying, the aircraft's loitering around the target area prior to target acquisition caused as much, if not more, anxiety since the Iraqi soldiers were unsure

Captain Swain's A-10 came home carrying the name CHOPPER POPPER and an Iraqi Flag kill marking for his helicoter kill. (Anthony Abbott)

of the chosen target." Another POW, an Iraqi Brigadier General whose unit was decimated by Warthogs, said that the A-10 had, "won the war" for the coalition forces and that his troops nicknamed the A-10 as "the silent gun."

DESERT STORM revived the old A-10 vs F-16 controversy and the data would be discussed at great lengths after the war during testimony in Congress. Both aircraft were used extensively in the war with substantial data on their success ratios of various types of missions. The F-16 had the advantage of speed and full night capabilities, whereas the A-10 required the use of flares to light up the battlefield or a second A-10. Yet despite these advantages, the F-16's performance in DESERT STORM was inferior to the A-10 in the Close-Air Support (CAS) role, primarily because the F-16 was extremely vulnerable to ground fire down low. It did not have the rugged survivability features that the A-10 had, consequently, the F-16 was forced to fly at higher altitudes. At night its Low Altitude Navigation for Night system (LANTERN) was far less effective at this altitude. At higher altitudes, the F-16's weapons were less accurate than the A-10's Maverick missile and gun strafing capabilities. The 30MM gun pod attachment for the F-16 proved to be unstable and inaccurate. The war had proved conclusively that the modified F-16 cannot replace the A-10 Warthog and perform all aspects of the CAS mission. The A-10 was truly the only aircraft that was built solely for the CAS mission. Many experts feel that the results of the war shows that the United States would do well to continue to have a mix of aircraft including the "air-to-mud" types.

One former Pentagon engineer, Pierre Sprey, who worked the F-16 and A-10 programs, was quoted in a Wall Street Journal article as saying that the idea of replacing the A-10 with the F-16 is, "one of the most monumentally fraudulent ideas that the Air Force has ever perpetrated." Mr. Sprey would later summarize the A-10's war accomplishments in the September 1991 issue of the IEEE Spectrum. He stated, "Among aircraft, the 'low tech' A-10 - much despised by U.S. Air Force brass - was the real hero of the air war. Even though it represent only one-twelfth of the fighter force, it flew one-third of the sorties and accounted for two-thirds of the tank kills claimed during the air campaign and better than nine/tenths of the artillery kills. It dominated the interdiction campaigns against the roads. The aircraft proved tough enough to survive the anti-aircraft exposure and fire anti-tank Maverick missiles, while the F-16s, F-111s and F-18s were just too vulnerable to ground guns to be usable in this role."

The A-10's participation in the Persian Gulf War continued the tradition where Fairchild-Republic aircraft have served in combat, which began with the P-47 in the Second World War. The A-10 lived up the official name of Thunderbolt II given in honor of the original Thunderbolt, the P-47.

The Future

Despite its success in DESERT STORM, the A-10 Warthog is not a sure thing to finish out the 20th Century as an active aircraft in the USAF inventory, either as an active duty or National Guard asset. A number of A-10s are planned to have night capabilities added through the use of a pod attachment to one of the underwing pylons. One improvement, Low Altitude Safety & Targeting Enhancement (LASTE) allowed the A-10 to win top honors at the 1992 Gunsmoke meet held by USAF attack units. Since the end of the war, the two main A-10 bases, Myrtle Beach AFB and England AFB, were recommended for closure by an independent commission, as part of the military downsizing. This downsizing is primarily due to the dissolution of the Warsaw Pact during the first half of 1991. These bases were closed in favor of a larger Air Force base that would include both A-10s and other aircraft. Over 100 A-10s have been placed in mothballs at Davis-Monthan AFB. The Air Force is keeping about 400 A-10s active in the inventory at this time. Recent events in the Gulf region had led to a number of A-10s being pre-positioned in Saudi Arabia to counter any future Iraqi threat. These aircraft will be maintained by contract personnel and will be kept combat ready, needing only crews and support personnel to be operational.

A proposal was made by the U.S. Forestry Service to purchase two A-10s and modifying them as water bombers to fight forest fires. The modifications would include the addition of a 1,500 gallon water tank to be carried under the aircraft centerline. The aircraft would be stripped of all weaponry and tactical avionics. At this time it appears doubtful that this proposal will be acted upon.

Since the war, there have been a number of inquires from several foreign countries in Asia, South America and the Middle East for A-10s. A deal was made with Turkey to take possession of 100 A-10s that were in storage at Davis-Monthan AFB. The original plan was that the transfer would take place over a period of three years. It is ironic that the plane is able to draw foreign interest now, after a war rather than when Republic

This A-10A of the 355th Tactical Fighter Wing is on final approach for landing at its home base at Davis Monthan AFB, Arizona. The aircraft is armed with AIM-9 Sidewinders, ECM pods and Maverick TV guided missiles. (Tony Sacketos)

Forrest Service A-10

A-10A

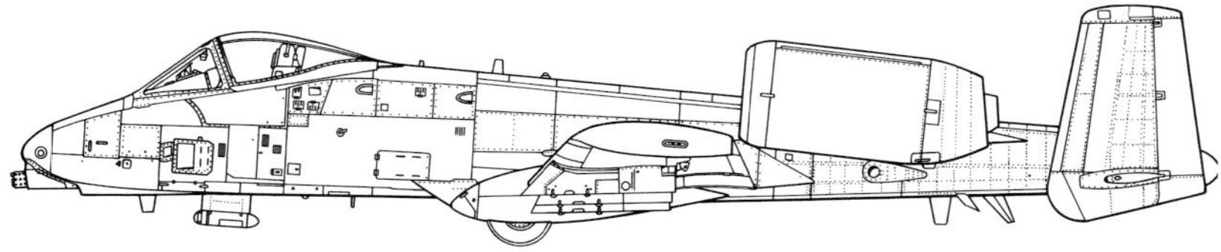

Proposed Tanker A-10

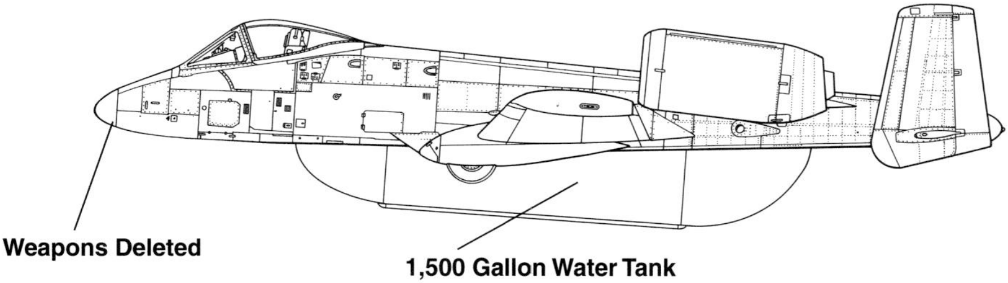

This OA-10 carries 2.75 inch rocket pods on the wing stations along with a Sidewinder air-to-air missile on the port outboard pylon. There appears to be a range instrumentation pod on the outboard starboard pylon. (Tony Sacketos)

A female Maryland National Guard armament crew member prepares to load the GAU-8 cannon of this 175th Fighter Group A-10A. The aircraft carries the unit badge on the engine nacelle in full color and a unit award ribbon on the fuselage just in front of the wing. (Rick Llinares)

The cockpit of the A-10 is rather simple, when compared to other USAF jet fighters. The screen at the right is the TV monitor for the Maverick missile system, the large circular instruments in the center of the panel are the attitude director indicator (top) and Horizontal Situation Indicator (bottom). (Ken Kubik)

This A-10A belongs to the 104th Fighter Squadron, 175th Fighter Group, Maryland Air National Guard at Martin Air Force Base, Baltimore, Maryland. This unit won the 1991 Gunsmoke gunnery competition. (RIck Llinares - Flight Line Photography)

The A-10 uses a single point refueling system with the hose attachment point housed in the port landing gear fairing. In addition, the fairing also houses a self-test panel to allow maintenance personnel to run checks on the aircraft's systems (RIck Llinares - Flight Line Photography)

A pair of A-10s of the Maryland Air National Guard fly a loose formation on a training mission. The aircraft are carrying twenty-five pound practice bombs on the fuselage stations and a Maverick TV guided missile on the inboard wing station. (RIck Llinares - Flight Line Photography)

was still in operation and had no luck in selling overseas. In any event, the Turkish deal fell through due to financial problems, not with the aircraft purchase, but rather with the support package.

The A-10's fate still seems to be tied to what happens with the F-16 aircraft in the fleet. Due to the fall of the Soviet Union, defense spending has been cut drastically and very few new programs are on the horizon. This includes the CAS version of the F-16 which is all but dead and it is probable that A-10s will be upgraded instead. It is probable too, that various USAF people, who will make the final decision, realize just how well this aircraft performed in the Gulf War and favor retention of the A-10 in the inventory. As one USAF source was quoted, "if the threat is reduced, the A-10's performance may be sufficient." The source also concluded, "Maybe the follow-on to the A-10 will be the A-10." Other sources also verified the fact that the A-10 fleet has aged well, since it was built to fighter specifications even though it is not typically flown like one. One such source states, "The A-10 is a damn tough aircraft, it was over-built for the way they've actually been flown." The years to come will be interesting to watch with regards to the A-10's continued service.

Recent events in the former Yugoslavia resulted in a squadron of A-10s being sent to the NATO airbase at Aviano, Italy. These A-10s were painted in the new Ghost Gray

(Right) The two small button antennas on either side of the nose are L band radar warning system antennas. The 30MM GAU-8 cannon has seven barrels that rotate through the firing chamber giving the weapon a rate of fire of either 2,100 rounds per minute or 4,200 rounds per minute. The round object at the lower left is the PAVE PENNY laser receiver pod that tracks any surface target illuminated by a laser (air or ground based), It outouts its data onto the HUD (visible in the center of the windscreen) and can also feed information directly to laser guided versions of the Maverick anti-armor guided missile. (RIck Llinares - Flight Line Photography)

A pair of A-10s prepare for takeoff on a training mission. These aircraft are in the European I camouflage scheme, with Black markings (except for rescue markings, which are in full color). (Tony Sacketos)

camouflage that is very similar to that carried by the A-10s early in the Warthog program. The A-10s saw action in support of UN peacekeepers against Serbian forces in 1993 and again in 1994. In the Sarajevo area, A-10s were used to destroy an M78 anti-tank gun after a UN weapon was seized by Serb forces. Reportedly the A-10s used some 600 rounds of 30MM fire to destroy the weapon.

A line-up of A-10As of the 172 Tactical Air Support Squadron, 110th Tactical Air Support Group, Michigan Air National Guard on the ramp at W.K. Kellogg Airport, Battle Creek, Michigan during 1993. (Tony Sacketos)

The A-10s of the 354th Fighter Squadron, 355th Fighter Wing at McCord Air Force Base, Washington carry a TC tail code (for Tacoma). The unit is in the process of changing over from European I camouflaged aircraft to Gray camouflage aircraft. (Tony Sacketos)

A formation of three aircraft from the 333rd Tactical Training Squadron, 355th Tactical Training Wing at Davis-Monthan Air Force Base, Arizona. The middle aircraft still carries the European I scheme, while the outboard aircraft are in the new Gray camouflage with a false canopy painted on the underside of the nose. (Tony Sacketos)

This A-10A carries a centerline pod painted in the markings of the 333rd Tactical Training Squaron. Other than the unit markings, all lettering is in Black. The aircraft carries an ECM pod, AIM-9 Sidewinder missiles and Gray painted Maverick anti-armor missiles. The checkerboard on the fin is in Red and White. (Tony Sacketos)

An A-10 of the 103rd Tactical Fighter Group, Connecticut Air National Guard undergoes an overhaul in the maintenance hangar at Bradley Air National Guard Base. (Ken Kubik)

An A-10 comes in for a landing at Davis-Monthan Air Force Base. The aircraft carries LAU-68 rocket pods on the wing pylons. These pods are used to carry 2.75 inch marker rockets, used to identify targets for other attack aircraft to destroy. (Tony Sacketos)

This A-10 belongs to the 131st Fighter Squadron, 104th Fighter Group, Massachusetts Air National Guard based at Barnes Municipal Airport, near Westfield, Massachusetts. This aircraft is named for the city and carries a map of the state on the nose in Black outlined in Yellow. (Ken Kubik)

Over the years a number of units have used Warthog nose art on their A-10s. This aircraft was assigned to the 46th Fighter Training Squadron, 917th Fighter Wing at Barksdale Air Force Base, Louisiana. (Ken Kubik)

A-10 tailcodes identify where the aircraft is based. The A-10 on the left (coded MD) is from the Maryland Air National Guard, while the aircraft on the right (coded CT) is from the Connecticut Air National Guard. (Ken Kubik)